DISCOVER EARTH SCIENCE

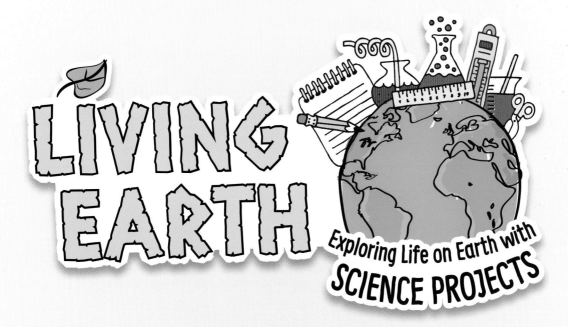

Exploring Life on Earth with
SCIENCE PROJECTS

by Suzanne Garbe

Raintree is an imprint of Capstone Global Library Limited, a company incorporated in England and Wales having its registered office at 7 Pilgrim Street, London, EC4V 6LB – Registered company number: 6695582

www.raintree.co.uk
myorders@raintree.co.uk

Edited by Alesha Sullivan
Designed by Sarah Bennett
Picture research by Kelly Garvin
Production by Lori Barbeau

ISBN 978 1 474 70326 0 (hardback)
19 18 17 16 15
10 9 8 7 6 5 4 3 2 1

ISBN 978 1 474 70331 4 (paperback)
20 19 18 17 16
10 9 8 7 6 5 4 3 2 1

British Library Cataloguing in Publication Data
A full catalogue record for this book is available from the British Library.

Acknowledgements
Capstone Press/Karon Dubke, 7, 9, 12, 13, 15, 18-19, 22, 23, 25, 28; Shutterstock: Evan Lorne, 10-11, focal point, 8, Jezper, 26-27, Jorg Hackemann, 24, Krivosheev Vitaly, 6-7, Konstantnin, 14, Marcio Jose Bastos Silva, 16-17, Natursports, 19 (top right), otsphoto, 4-5, R.L.Hausdorf, 20-21, sittitap, cover, snapgalleria, 6 (bottom right), Stephen Tucker, 29, Studio_G, 27 (inset)
Design Elements: Shutterstock: Curly Pat, Magnia, Markovka, Ms.Moloko, Orfeev, pockygallery, Sashatigar, Żabrotskaya Larisa

We would like to thank Daniel S. Jones, Research Associate with the Department of Earth Sciences and BioTechnology Institute at the University of Minnesota, for his invaluable help in the preparation of this book.

Printed and bound in China.

Contents

Life on Earth

What does it mean to be alive and active? A game of football or netball is certainly active. So is a dog chasing a ball. And plants inside a greenhouse with their leaves angled towards the Sun are living, too.

But what about the green stuff growing on rocks at the bottom of lakes? Or the carton of milk that's starting to smell unpleasant? What processes are responsible for the way our planet works? What invisible things are happening to the world around us?

Dive into experiments and explore some of the principles behind our living Earth using ordinary household items. Some of these experiments may require an adult's help. But you can do most of them on your own. If things get messy, just remember to clean up. It's time to roll up your sleeves and get your hands dirty!

Into the darkness

Plants are essential to life on Earth. Like you, plants also need food to live. They have a unique way of getting food. Through **photosynthesis**, most plants are able to make their own food. **Chlorophyll** is very important to the process. Chlorophyll is also what gives plants their green colour. But what happens when chlorophyll can't access sunlight? You can discover the answer to this question using a few simple materials.

Cycle of plant life

Plants need light, water and **carbon dioxide** for photosynthesis to take place. During photosynthesis plants release oxygen into the air. That's where animals and humans get oxygen to breathe. When animals and humans breathe in oxygen, they breathe out carbon dioxide and water. This process is known as **respiration** and is the opposite of photosynthesis. Together they form a cycle that supports most life on Earth.

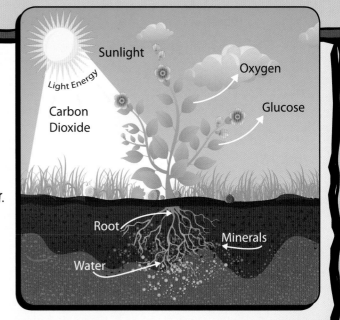

Sunlight

Light Energy

Oxygen

Glucose

Carbon Dioxide

Root

Minerals

Water

What you do

What you need

indoor plant with large leaves

black construction paper

tape

water

1. Buy a small indoor plant or choose one already in your house. Make sure it has large leaves.

2. Put the plant on a sunny window-sill.

3. Wrap black construction paper around one leaf of the plant. Tape it in place.

4. Water the plant according to the directions that came with the plant.

5. Remove the construction paper after one week.

How does the leaf you covered look compared to the other leaves? How did the construction paper affect the chlorophyll?

photosynthesis process by which green plants make their food

chlorophyll green substance in plants that uses light to make food from carbon dioxide and water

carbon dioxide colourless, odourless gas that people and animals breathe out

respiration process of taking in oxygen and sending out carbon dioxide

"Watering" plants

Plants grow differently depending on their environments. Soil type, temperature, sunlight and water are all factors that can affect plant growth. But what about the type of water? House plants are usually watered from a sink. Outdoor plants often survive on rainwater. Maybe water isn't the only thing that can make a plant grow. What would happen if you gave a plant a drink meant for humans, such as lemonade or orange juice?

environment   natural world of the land, water and air

What you do

1. Use your pen to poke a small hole in the bottom of each cup.

2. Half fill each cup with potting soil.

3. Put three seeds into each cup. Follow the seed packet's instructions about how deeply to plant each seed.

4. Write labels for two cups to show what type of liquid you will use on each plant. The third cup should be labelled "water". Tape the labels onto the cups.

5. Place the cups onto the tray. Put the tray on a sunny window-sill.

6. Water each plant with 80 millilitres of liquid for each labelled cup.

7. Continue to water each cup every other day with 80 millilitres of liquid. If a lot of liquid seeps out from the cup, you can reduce the amount.

8. Record in your notebook when a shoot first appears in each cup.

What differences do you notice between the plants? How did the liquid you chose for each cup affect the plants' growth? Were there any cups where no plants grew at all?

What you need

pen

3 paper cups

potting soil

9 seeds for the same vegetable or flower of your choice

paper labels

2 liquids of your choice, such as juice or lemonade

water

tape

tray to hold the cups

sunny window-sill

measuring jug

paper or notebook for taking notes

Compost jars

If you've ever gardened, you may have heard of **compost**. It is made from organic matter such as leaves, grass clippings, fruit peels or coffee grounds. Compost is created when bacteria and fungi cause the materials to rot and break down. The process is an important part of the food chain. Once a plant dies, something has to help that plant **decompose**. Then it becomes compost, which helps new life grow. Many people spread compost in their gardens to help plants grow better.

compost mixture of rotten leaves, vegetables, manure and other items that are added to soil to make it richer

decompose rot or decay

Not everything can be composted. Some things take too long to break down. Which items break down quickly? What types of conditions help this process? Beware, compost can get very smelly!

How long to decompose?

Banana peel ➡	3-4 weeks
Cardboard ➡	2 months
Plastic bags ➡	Between months and hundreds of years
Aluminum can ➡	200 years
Disposable nappies ➡	500 years
Polystyrene ➡	1 million years

FACT

Between 20 and 30 per cent of what we throw in the bin can be composted. Composting is good because it helps create healthy soil and reduces the amount of rubbish in landfills. Some people have compost bins in their gardens.

What you do

What you need

soil collected from a garden, park or field

3 clear jars or bottles of a similar shape and size

fruit scraps (banana peel, orange peel, apple core etc.)

5-centimetre (2-in) piece of polystyrene or plastic

1 piece of paper, torn into strips

measuring spoons

water

spoon or fork

sunny window-sill

pen and paper or notebook for taking notes

1. Add soil to each jar or bottle until each is half full.

2. Put fruit scraps in a jar, the piece of polystyrene or plastic in another, and a few strips of paper in the third.

3. Add 15 millilitres of water to each jar. Mix everything together.

4. Leave the lids off and place the jars on a sunny window-sill in a well-**ventilated** room. Take notes about what you see every day. Include information such as the size, shape and colour of any objects you can see as the mixture begins to turn into compost.

5. After one week, add 15 millilitres of water to each jar and mix the contents. Record any changes you notice.

6. Continue the experiment for another couple of weeks if you wish. Repeat step 5 after each week.

You should see that the fruit scraps and paper start to decompose, while the plastic or polystyrene does not. Why is this? What is the connection between what you observed and the items people chose to compost?

ventilate allow fresh air in and send stale air out

How fast do things decompose in landfills?

For something to decompose, certain conditions are necessary. Bacteria, fungi, water, sunlight and heat all make decomposition possible. But many landfills are packed too tightly for the right conditions to be present. That's why items in a landfill might decompose much more slowly than they do in your window-sill experiment. Researchers from Michigan State University, USA, decided to dig into a landfill and look at old rubbish. They found grass clippings and several hot dogs that were more than 30 years old. They even found a 30-year-old newspaper that was still readable.

Earth's layers

The top layers of Earth are called **sedimentary** layers. They are like a book that tells the history of life on our planet. The sediment that makes up the layers can be as small as a piece of dirt or as large as a boulder.

Sedimentation can be a helpful process. When rivers move sediment downstream, the sediment often adds good **nutrients** to the soil. That's why the land beside rivers is often great farmland. Now it's your turn to experiment with sedimentation!

sediment   tiny bits of rock, shells, plants, sand and minerals that settle at the bottom of a liquid

nutrient   substance needed by a living thing to stay healthy

What you do

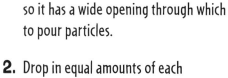

1. Cut the top off the plastic bottle so it has a wide opening through which to pour particles.

2. Drop in equal amounts of each of the three natural particles you collected.

3. Pour water into the bottle until it covers the particles and stops about 10 centimetres (4 in) above the particles.

4. Place the bottle in a sunny window. Stir the materials with the plastic spoon or stick so they are well-mixed. Be careful not to spill anything.

5. Make notes about what the particles look like after one minute, 30 minutes and 24 hours.

   Look at the layers formed inside the bottle. Which particles settled at the bottom most quickly? Which ended up on top? How do the weight and size of each particle type influence how quickly the particles settle to the bottom?

What you need

scissors

clean, empty plastic bottle or milk carton

240 millilitres each of three natural particles of different sizes, such as sand, dirt, small pebbles or rocks

water

sunny window

plastic spoon or stick

pen and paper or notebook for taking notes

clock or timer

Make your own fossils!

Fossils have helped us learn much of what we know about past life on Earth. They show us how long different life forms have been around and how those life forms lived in the past. They can even teach us about plants and animals that no longer exist. Fossils can also tell us about what the planet used to look like.

fossil remains or traces of plants and animals that are preserved as rock

Sometimes fossils are the remains of living things, such as bones, teeth and wood. Fossils can also be the imprint of something, such as a foot or a leaf that is no longer there. How are fossils made? Make your own and find out!

What you do

What you need

120 millilitres used, wet coffee grounds

120 millilitres cold coffee

120 grams salt

120 grams flour

baking or parchment paper

4 different objects, such as a leaf, a twig, a small toy or your foot

1. Mix together the coffee grounds, coffee, salt and flour. It should form a dough-like substance.

2. Divide the dough into four chunks.

3. Flatten each chunk onto a sheet of baking or parchment paper.

4. Press one object into each of your flattened chunks of dough. Then remove the object.

5. Let the mixture dry overnight.

6. Now show your fossil imprints to your family or friends!

Can your family or friends tell which object made each fossil? One thousand years from now, what might your fossil imprints tell people about the place where you live?

Palaeontology

For decades **palaeontologists** have used tools such as hammers, picks and brushes to clear away dirt and dig up fossils. Palaeontologists also use advanced tools such as microscopes and computers. Fossils can tell us information about what the planet was like thousands of years ago. Fossils also allow scientists to predict how the environment will change and impact life in the future.

palaeontologist scientist who studies fossils

Home-made salt flats

Salt flats are big, flat stretches of land covered with salt and other **minerals**. Salt flats are the result of **evaporation** from a former body of water. This would be similar to plugging your sink and then filling it with water. The water can't drain away, so it stays there until it evaporates. In a salt flat, while the water is evaporating, salt and minerals that are in the water stay behind.

Salt flats are an example of how the living Earth is always changing. The Bonneville Salt Flats in Utah, USA, were once a lake twice the size of Wales. And it's possible that as weather patterns change, a salt flat could flood and become a lake once again. Try to make your own miniature salt flat using a few common items!

mineral solid substance found in nature that is produced by natural processes

evaporate change from a liquid to a vapour or a gas

FACT

The Bonneville Salt Flats in Utah, USA, are one of the best-known salt flats in the world. Many films, including *Pirates of the Caribbean: At World's End*, have been filmed there. The Bonneville Salt Flats even have their own racetrack, the Bonneville Speedway!

What you do

What you need

- large mixing bowl
- spoon for stirring
- measuring jug
- salt
- hot water
- measuring spoons
- bicarbonate of soda
- potting soil
- glass baking dish
- pen and paper or notebook for taking notes

1. In a bowl, stir 120 grams of salt into 240 millilitres of hot water until the salt dissolves.

2. Add 15 grams of bicarbonate of soda and 15 grams of soil. Stir again.

3. Pour the mixture into a glass baking dish. Let the dish sit for a few days until the water has evaporated. Take notes on the colour and **texture** of the mixture.

4. Repeat step 1 again. Pour the new mixture on top of the dried mixture. Let it dry for a few days.

5. Repeat steps 1 and 2, using 120 grams of salt, 240 millilitres of hot water, 80 grams of bicarbonate of soda and 80 grams of soil. Pour the new mixture on top of the dried mixture. Let it dry for a few more days. Take notes on the colour and texture of all of the layers.

6. Repeat two or three times with different amounts of bicarbonate of soda and soil each time. Take notes about the look and texture of each layer.

What do you notice about the look and feel of each layer? Why do you think nothing grows in a salt flat?

texture way something feels when you touch it

A watery planet

About 97 per cent of the water on Earth is salt water. It is important for the many creatures that live in the sea. Humans and many other animals, however, need freshwater to survive. But many countries have experienced water shortages in recent years. Some parts of the United States, including California and Arizona, have water shortages. One potential solution is to use **desalination** to turn salt water into freshwater.

Some countries — including Saudi Arabia, Israel and Singapore — already use desalination. Now you can see how this process works without leaving your house!

FACT

Desalination is not an environmentally friendly process. A desalination plant uses three times the amount of energy that a normal water treatment plant uses. It also requires chemicals that may harm the sea.

What you do

What you need

measuring jug

water

2 cereal bowls

measuring spoons

table salt

spoon for stirring

drinking straw

clay

large mixing bowl

cling film

large rubber band

small rock

sunny window-sill

1. Pour 475 millilitres water into a cereal bowl. Add 30 grams salt and stir until salt is **dissolved**.

2. With the straw, take a small sip of water and spit it out. It should taste salty. Don't swallow!

3. Flatten a piece of clay and put it in the bottom of the mixing bowl.

4. Pour the salt water into the mixing bowl until the water is about 2.5 centimetres (1 in) high.

5. Place the second cereal bowl into the mixing bowl and press it into the clay. The cereal bowl should be higher than the water but below the top of the mixing bowl. The cereal bowl should be dry inside.

6. Wrap cling film over the top of the mixing bowl. Let the cling film sag a little into the bowl but not touch the water or bowl. Hold the cling film in place by wrapping the rubber band around the mixing bowl just below the rim.

7. Place the rock on the middle of the cling film so the cling film dips towards the cereal bowl.

8. Put the mixing bowl on a sunny window-sill for a day or two.

You should notice some water has collected in the cereal bowl. Take a sip of this water. What can you taste?

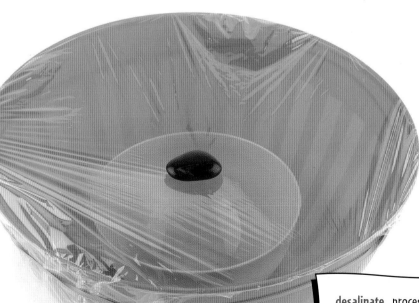

desalinate process of removing salt from water

dissolve seeming to disappear when mixed with liquid

25

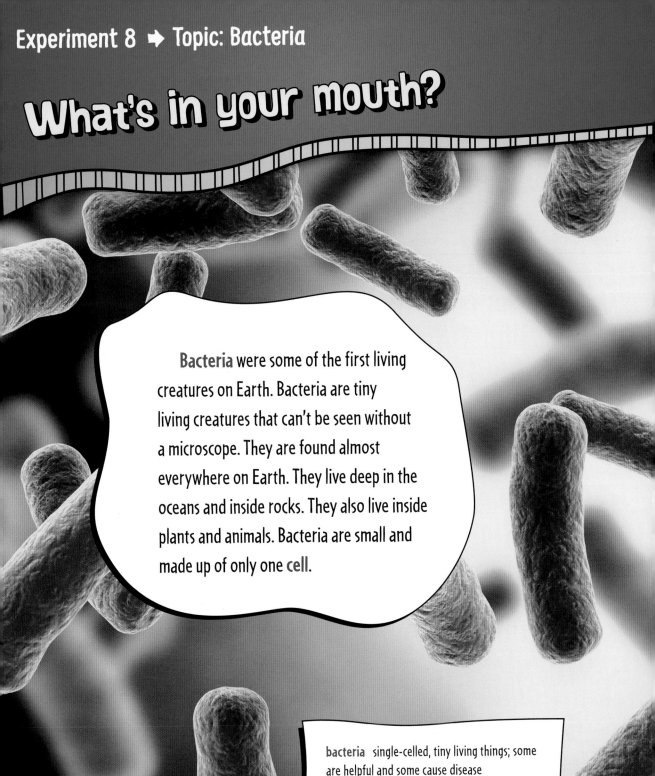

What's in your mouth?

Bacteria were some of the first living creatures on Earth. Bacteria are tiny living creatures that can't be seen without a microscope. They are found almost everywhere on Earth. They live deep in the oceans and inside rocks. They also live inside plants and animals. Bacteria are small and made up of only one **cell**.

bacteria single-celled, tiny living things; some are helpful and some cause disease

cell smallest part of a living thing

Some bacteria are helpful to people. We have good bacteria that live inside our bodies and help us process food. Other kinds of bacteria are used to help ripen cheese and make medicine.

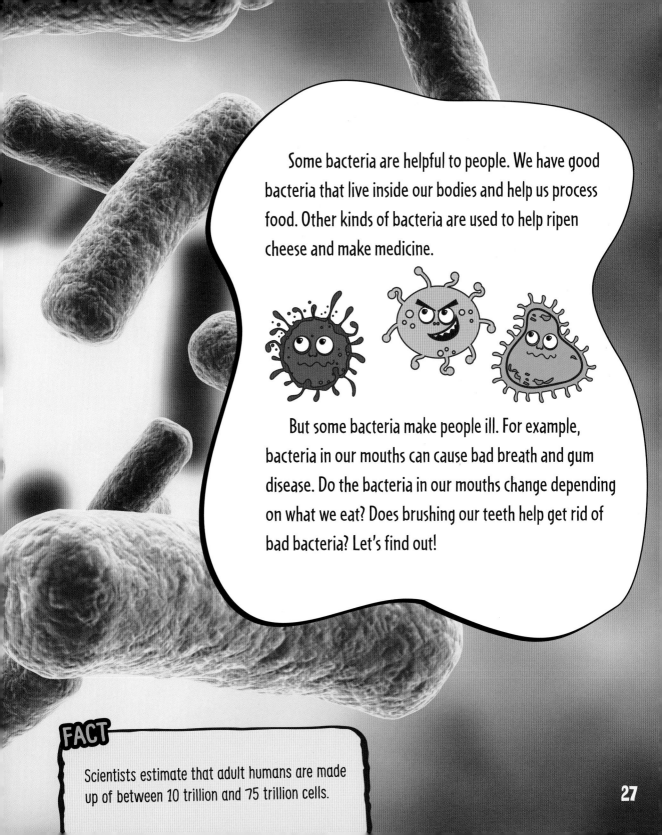

But some bacteria make people ill. For example, bacteria in our mouths can cause bad breath and gum disease. Do the bacteria in our mouths change depending on what we eat? Does brushing our teeth help get rid of bad bacteria? Let's find out!

FACT

Scientists estimate that adult humans are made up of between 10 trillion and 75 trillion cells.

What you do

1. Label the agar plates "control", "sweet" and "bread".

2. Brush your teeth with toothpaste, and rinse your mouth with water.

3. Rub a cotton swab against the inside of your cheek. Then wipe it across the agar plate marked "control" so your saliva forms a line down the plate.

4. Eat the sweet.

5. Repeat step 3 using the agar plate marked "sweet".

6. Brush your teeth and rinse your mouth again. Then eat the piece of bread.

7. Repeat step 3 using the agar plate marked "bread".

8. Put the lids on the agar plates, tape them shut and put them in a dark cupboard.

9. After 24 hours look at each plate and record what you see. Include information such as the number and size of any visible bacteria growth.

10. Make notes again after two days, three days and four days.

What can you see in each plate? You should see bacteria growing. The dish marked "sweet" should have the most bacteria. What does this suggest about the role of sugar in helping bacteria grow? Why is it important to brush your teeth?

What you need

pen

3 sticky labels

3 prepared **agar plates**

toothbrush

toothpaste

water

3 cotton swabs

a sweet

piece of bread

tape

dark place, such as a cupboard

paper or notebook for
    taking notes

plastic bag

agar plate small clear dish filled with a gel that helps microscopic things grow

Extraordinary Earth

You don't need expensive laboratory equipment to understand how the natural world works. Life on Earth involves amazing cycles of growth and decay. If you know where to look, every day brings you into contact with these living processes. From dead leaves to young plants to desert sands, the planet is changing and living, just like we are.

Glossary

agar plate small clear dish filled with a gel that helps microscopic things grow

bacteria single-celled, tiny living things; some are helpful and some cause disease

carbon dioxide colourless, odourless gas that people and animals breathe out

cell smallest part of a living thing

chlorophyll green substance in plants that uses light to make food from carbon dioxide and water

compost mixture of rotten leaves, vegetables, manure and other items that are added to soil to make it richer

decompose rot or decay

desalinate process of removing salt from water

dissolve seeming to disappear when mixed with liquid

environment natural world of the land, water and air

evaporate change from a liquid to a vapour or a gas

fossil remains or traces of plants and animals that are preserved as rock

mineral solid substance found in nature that is produced by natural processes

nutrient substance needed by a living thing to stay healthy

palaeontologist scientist who studies fossils

photosynthesis process by which green plants make their food

respiration process of taking in oxygen and sending out carbon dioxide

sediment tiny bits of rock, shells, plants, sand and minerals that settle at the bottom of a liquid

texture way something feels when you touch it

ventilate allow fresh air in and send stale air out

Read more

101 Way to Save the Planet (101 Ways), Deborah Underwood (Raintree, 2012)

Getting Rid of Waste (Headline Issues), Angela Royston (Raintree, 2010)

How Does a Bone Become a Fossil? (How Does It Happen?), Melissa Stewart (Raintree, 2011)

Life Processes (Essential Life Science), Richard & Louise Spilsbury (Raintree, 2014)

Websites

www.bbc.co.uk/bitesize/ks2/science/living_things/
Uncover the secret world of microorganisms and other life processes through games, quizzes, diagrams and film.

http://ngkids.co.uk/science-and-nature/
Did you know that about 70 per cent of the oxygen we breathe is produced by Earth's oceans? For more amazing facts about Earth processes, and some fascinating deep sea photography, visit the National Geographic children's website.

Index